MW01609492

# Remember When…?

Remember FDR and Winston Churchill? How about Frank Sinatra,
The King of Swoon, and Rosie the Riveter?
If you can remember when swallowing goldfish was common,
or when the Stork Club was uncommonly cool…

*Then you must be ready for a 40s party!*

**THIS BOOK OF MEMORIES PRESENTED TO:**

_____

**ON THE OCCASION OF:**

_____

**DATE:**

# SETTING THE SCENE

## 1940

- Gas is 19¢ a gallon
- Rockefeller Center opens in New York City
- The German Luftwaffe launches 652 bombers on London (the Blitz)

## 1941

- The Japanese attack Pearl Harbor: "a date which will live in infamy"
- Walt Disney's career takes off with *Fantasia* (1940) and *Dumbo* (1941)
- The Manhattan Project begins

## 1942

- The internment of Japanese Americans begins
- Japan murders 250,000 Chinese civilians in retaliation for aid given to US
- Gas chambers at Auschwitz begin operation
- Enrico Fermi reports the first nuclear reaction

## 1943

- The Jefferson Memorial is opened in Washington DC
- 16,000 POWs and 80,000 Asian slave laborers die during the construction of a Japanese railway between Thailand and Burma

## 1944

- Allied forces land in Normandy to begin the invasion of western Europe (D-Day)
- *Seventeen* magazine begins publication
- Civil war erupts in Greece
- The World Bank and the International Monetary Fund are created

## 1945

- FDR is sworn in for an unprecedented fourth term as president of the US
- America tests an atomic bomb at Los Alamos, New Mexico
- Germany surrenders: V-E Day 5/8/45
- Bess Myerson is the first college graduate to become Miss America
- America drops atomic bombs on Hiroshima & then Nagasaki
- Japan surrenders: V-J day 8/14/45
- The United Nations is created in San Francisco

## 1946

- First year of the Baby Boom
- Trials of high-ranking Nazi officers are held in Nuremberg, Germany
- Communists, led by Mao Zedong, take over the government of China

 ## 1948

- The Soviet Union invades Czechoslovakia
- Congress approves the Marshall Plan, an economic aid plan which rebuilds Europe
- The Soviet Union blockades all land routes to Berlin, resulting in the Berlin Airlift
- The independent nation of Israel is proclaimed
- The Irish Free State becomes the Republic of Ireland

## 1947

- Thor Heyerdahl sails the Kon-Tiki from Peru to Polynesia
- Chuck Yaeger breaks the sound barrier
- The House Un-American Activities Committee hearings get underway
- The UN partitions the country of Palestine into Jewish and Arab states
- Pan Am introduces the first round-the-world flight

 ## 1949

- NATO is formed in response to Soviet aggression
- The Soviets explode their first atomic bomb
- East and West Germany are established

# The Buzz

BIG APPLE

ENOLA GAY

FIORELLO LAGUARDIA

IL DUCE

PINUP GIRLS

EDWARD R. MURROW

THE SPRUCE GOOSE

FALA

ROBERTA CAPA

ELEANOR ROOSEVELT

THE STAGE DOOR CANTEEN

ANNE FRANK

TOOTS SHOR'S

WILLIE & JOE

MOVIETONE NEWS

"KILROY WAS HERE"

# TOP OF THE CHARTS

**Boogie Woogie Bugle Boy**
Andrews Sisters

**Mañana**
Peggy Lee

**In the Blue of the Evening**
Tommy Dorsey

**All or Nothing at All**
Frank Sinatra

**Paper Doll**
The Mills Brothers

**Frenesi**
Artie Shaw

**I'll Never Smile Again**
Tommy Dorsey with Frank Sinatra

**Chattanooga Choo Choo**
Glenn Miller

**In the Mood**
Glenn Miller

**You'd be So Nice to Come Home To**
Frank Sinatra

**Amapola**
Jimmy Dorsey

**Daddy**
Sammy Kaye

**Kalamazoo**
Glenn Miller

**Buttons and Bows**
Dinah Shore

**White Christmas**
Bing Crosby

**Shoo-Shoo Baby**
Andrews Sisters

## The Buzz

FATS WALLER

LES BROWN ORCHESTRA

THE LATIN QUARTER

BENNY GOODMAN, KING OF SWING

BIG BAND SOUND

LENA HORNE    LICORICE STICK    CARMEN MIRANDA

RADIO CITY MUSIC HALL    DUKE ELLINGTON

CHARLIE PARKER & BE-BOP JAZZ

RUM AND COCA COLA
Andrews Sisters

SENTIMENTAL JOURNEY
Les Brown with Doris Day

'TIL THE END OF TIME
Perry Como

SWINGING ON A STAR
Bing Crosby

ON THE ATCHISON, TOPEKA
AND THE SANTA FE
Johnny Mercer

MULE TRAIN
Frankie Laine

I DON'T WANT TO SET
THE WORLD ON FIRE
Horace Heidt

YOU'RE BREAKING MY HEART
Vic Damone

SOME ENCHANTED EVENING
Perry Como

I'VE HEARD THAT SONG BEFORE
Harry James

MOONLIGHT COCKTAIL
Glenn Miller

CARE TO DANCE?

the Jitterbug

the Tango

the Bolero

the Rhumba

the Lindy Hop

# WHAT TELEVISION?

Fibber McGee & Molly

Information Please

Take It or Leave It

Truth or Consequences

Quiz Kids

Kay Kyser, the Ol' Professor

Lux Radio Theater

Edgar Bergen & Charlie McCarthy

Columbia Workshop

The Goldbergs

Duffy's Tavern

One Man's Family

Jack Benny

Fred Allen

Kate Smith

Arthur Godfrey

## That New-Fangled Television!

**Texaco Star Theater**

**Howdy Doody**

**The Original Amateur Hour**

**Kukla, Fran & Ollie**

Gooney Bird

Schnozz

Number One Son

Gung Ho

Canary

Jerry Can

Dogface

Snow Job

Copacetic

Dukes

Noggin

Swell

Baby

Jake

Kicks

Birdbrain

Daddy-O

S.O.P.

Choppers

JIVE

Doll/Dame/Angelcake

Vamoose

Plant You Now & Dig You Later

Hepcat/Hepkitten

See 'Ya Later Alligator (After While Crocodile)

Jungle Juice

Ticker

Flip Your Lid

Threads

We Had a Ball

Gangbusters

Slang of the 40s

# MOVIES WE HAD TO SEE

- ✦ Gone With the Wind
- ✕ The Great Dictator
- ✦ It's a Wonderful Life
- ✕ Citizen Kane
- ✦ The Treasure of the Sierra Madre
- ✕ The Road to Morocco
- ✦ Lassie Come Home
- ✕ The Miracle on 34th Street
- ✦ Going My Way
- ✕ Double Indemnity
- ✦ Gaslight
- ✕ Meet Me in St. Louis
- ✦ National Velvet
- ✕ The Picture of Dorian Gray

- ✦ Mildred Pierce
- ✕ State Fair
- ✦ The Postman Always Rings Twice
- ✕ The Big Sleep
- ✦ Yankee Doodle Dandy
- ✕ Twelve O'Clock High
- ✦ The Philadelphia Story
- ✕ Kitty Foyle
- ✦ Meet John Doe
- ✕ Suspicion
- ✦ Flying Tigers
- ✕ All the King's Men
- ✦ The Maltese Falcon
- ✕ Gentleman's Agreement
- ✦ Woman of the Year

# PERSONALITIES

Abbott & Costello

Bette Davis

Betty Grable

Joan Crawford

Cary Grant

Rita Hayworth

Jimmy Cagney

Hedda Hopper

Katherine Hepburn

Bing Crosby

Bob Hope

Cary Grant

Humphrey Bogart
& Lauren Bacall

Ingrid Bergman

Orson Welles

Spencer Tracy

Fred Astaire

Mickey Rooney

Clark Gable
& Carole Lombard

Grauman's Chinese Theatre

Charlie Chan

Jimmy Stewart

Roy Rogers
& Dale Evans

## *Academy Award® Best Pictures*

| 1940 | Rebecca | 1945 | The Lost Weekend |
|------|---------|------|------------------|
| 1941 | How Green Was My Valley | 1946 | The Best Years of Our Lives |
| 1942 | Mrs. Miniver | 1947 | Gentleman's Agreement |
| 1943 | Casablanca | 1948 | Hamlet |
| 1944 | Going My Way | 1949 | All the King's Men |

# ON BROADWAY

A STREETCAR NAMED DESIRE

*

OKLAHOMA!

*

**Glass Menagerie**

*

CAROUSEL

*

BRIGADOON

*

**Death of a Salesman**

*

SOUTH PACIFIC

*

KISS ME, KATE

*

**Annie Get Your Gun**

# ON THE COFFEE TABLE

Joe Palooke

Blondie

Lil' Abner

Little Orphan Annie

Dick Tracy

# ON THE BOOKSHELF

- *The Egg and I* – *Betty MacDonald*
- *Life* magazine
- *Forever Amber* – *Kathleen Winsor*
- *The Robe* – *Lloyd C. Douglas*
- *The Black Rose* – *Thomas B. Costain*
- *Guadalcanal Diary* – *Richard Tregaskis*
- *A Tree Grows in Brooklyn* – *Betty Smith*
- *They Were Expendable* – *William L. White*
- *Brave Men* – *Ernie Pyle*
- *Up Front* – *Bill Mauldin*
- *Cannery Row* – *John Steinbeck*
- *Common Sense Book of Baby and Child Care* – *Dr. Benjamin Spock*

*The Gumps*

*Gasoline Alley*

*Moon Mullins*

*Bringing Up Father*

*Terry and the Pirates*

*The Funny Papers*

# WHERE WERE YOU WHEN...

## 1940

- Germany invades Norway, Denmark, Belgium, Luxembourg, the Netherlands, France
- Italy joins the Axis and enters the war on the side of Germany
- Germany creates a Jewish ghetto in Warsaw, Poland

## 1941

- The Japanese attack Pearl Harbor

## 1942

- Manila falls to the Japanese; Gen. MacArthur leaves the Philippines, vowing, "I shall return"
- As many as 20,000 Allied prisoners die on the Bataan Death March
- Allied forces win the battle for Midway Island, and go on to take Guadalcanal
- Allied troops under British General Montgomery invade North Africa

## 1943

- The Allies take Tunisia, and launch an invasion of Sicily
- The Jews of Warsaw stage an uprising; later the ghetto is completely destroyed
- The tide of the Pacific war begins to turn as Allied troops island hop toward Japan

## 1944

- Americans liberate Rome
- France is liberated after four years of German occupation
- Allied troops hold firm at the Battle of the Bulge, Germany's last offensive

## 1945

- MacArthur returns to the Philippines, and Allied forces wage a fierce battle for Manila
- Marines raise the American flag on Iwo Jima
- The bombing of Dresden creates a firestorm that rages for a week and levels the city
- Allied troops cross the Rhine and enter Germany
- American troops liberate Buchenwald; American journalists are there to record the atrocities
- FDR dies

ALGER HISS
FOXHOLE
CONCENTRATION CAMPS
FIRESIDE CHATS
NAZIS
AIR RAIDS
HOLOCAUST
V FOR VICTORY

## 1946

- George Marshall envisions a plan to promote the economic recovery of European democracies
- There are 250,000 Displaced Persons in European refugee camps

## 1947

- The "Truman Doctrine" (containing the expansion of communism) is announced

## 1948

- India and Pakistan gain independence from Britain
- Gandhi is assassinated

## 1949

- Communists led by Mao Zedong seize power in China
- The communist insurgency in Greece ends

# The Buzz

AUDIE MURPHY

THE THIRD REICH

JOHN HERSEY

U-BOATS

ACK-ACK

ZERO

OMAHA BEACH BLITZKRIEG

GI BILL

KAMIKAZE PILOTS

THE SS

FLYING FORTRESS

ELEANOR ROOSEVELT

DOOLITTLE'S RAID

GOLD STAR MOTHERS

QUONSET HUT

FÜHRER

NAVAJO CODE TALKERS

THE BLACKSHIRTS

ESSENTIAL WORKER

"LOOSE LIPS SINK SHIPS"

FASCISTS

WAR BOND RALLIES

GASOLINE RATIONING

BLACKOUTS / BROWNOUTS / DIMOUTS

(A, B, AND C WINDSHIELD STICKERS)

WACs / WAVES

THE USO

"WE'RE IN IT – LET'S WIN IT"

VICTORY VOLUNTEERS

VICTORY GARDENS

LUFTWAFFE

# What We Wore

Rolled up blue jeans & boys' shirttails

WHITE SOCKS AND LOAFERS

**Zoot Suits (with widebrimmed hats and long watch chain)**

Saddle Shoes

OPEN TOED SHOES

Ankle Straps

**Peplums and Ruffles**

PEGGED PANTS

High Heeled Shoes

Tropical Styles / Cuban Heels

NYLONS BEGIN REPLACING SILK STOCKINGS

Ducktail Haircut

**Women began to wear pants in public**

SNOODS AND TURBANS

Cashmere Sweaters

Padded Shoulders

WOMEN'S CONVERTIBLE DAY-TO-EVENING SUITS

BIKINI SWIMSUITS

**Home Permanents**

# How We Traveled

* BY TRAIN *(the Twentieth Century Limited, the Zephyr)*
* BY PLANE *(Pan Am's luxury flights on the Yankee Clipper)*
* SOMETIMES BY AUTOMOBILE *(De Soto, Cadillac, the Cord)*

# Popular Vacation Desinations

* Rio de Janeiro
* the Caribbean
* Coney Island
* the South Pacific *(Fiji, New Caledonia, New Zealand)*

## The Buzz

STEWARDESS

DRIVE-IN THEATERS

LUNCH COUNTERS

"WHICH TWIN HAS THE TONI?"

CARHOPS

COUNTY & STATE FAIRS

JUKEBOX MUSIC

CIVVIES

FULLER BRUSH MAN

BOBBYSOXERS

DEAR JOHN LETTER

CANASTA

SILLY PUTTY

ERECTOR SETS

SCRABBLE

GENERAL STORES

# Food and Drink Trends

Pineapple
Upside Down Cake

CASSEROLES

Rum
Cocktails

Prepared
Cake Mixes

Pot Roast

Frozen Food

Goopy
Desserts

Tropical
Punch

CHIQUITA®
BANANA

M & Ms®

CHEERIOS®

Chiffon Cake

Margarine

## Sloppy Joes

**1 lb.** Hamburger
**1** Onion, chopped
**1 T.** Mustard
**1 T.** Brown sugar

**1 t.** Salt
**1** Dash of ground cloves
**1c.** Catsup

In large pan, brown hamburger and onion. Drain fat and return to pan. Add remaining ingredients. Simmer over low heat at least one hour, stirring occasionally. Serve on hamburger buns.

## Mai Tai

**1 ½ oz.** dark rum
**½ oz. each:** orange curacao, creme de noyaux, and lime juice
Dash of grenadine if desired

Shake with ice and serve in a Hurricane or decorative glass. Garnish with skewered orange slice and cherry.

# Who Won the World Series in...

|  |  |
|------|--------|
| **1940** | Cincinnati Reds 4, Detroit Tigers 3 |
| **1941** | New York Yankees 4, Brooklyn Dodgers 1 |
| **1942** | St. Louis Cardinals 4, New York Yankees 1 |
| **1943** | New York Yankees 4, St. Louis Cardinals 1 |
| **1944** | St. Louis Cardinals 4, St. Louis Browns, 2 |
| **1945** | Detroit Tigers 4, Chicago Cubs 3 |
| **1946** | St. Louis Cardinals 4, Boston Red Sox 3 |
| **1947** | New York Yankees 4, Brooklyn Dodgers 3 |
| **1948** | Cleveland Indians 4, Boston Braves 2 |
| **1949** | New York Yankees 4, Brooklyn Dodgers 1 |

# Who Won the NFL Championship in...

|  |  |
|------|--------|
| **1940** | Chicago Bears 73, Washington Redskins 0 |
| **1941** | Chicago Bears 37, New York Giants 9 |
| **1942** | Washington Redskins 14, Chicago Bears 6 |
| **1943** | Chicago Bears 41, Washington Redskins 21 |
| **1944** | Green Bay Packers 14, New York Giants 7 |
| **1945** | Cleveland Browns 15, Washington Redskins 14 |
| **1946** | Chicago Bears 24, New York Giants 14 |
| **1947** | Chicago Cardinals 28, Philadelphia Eagles 21 |
| **1948** | Philadelphia Eagles 7, Chicago Cardinals 0 |
| **1949** | Philadelphia Eagles 14, Los Angeles Rams 0 |

## Who Won the NBA Championship in...

*NBA did not exist before 1946*

**1947** ...............Philadelphia Warriors 4, Chicago Stags 1
**1948** ............Baltimore Bullets 4, Philadelphia Warriors 2
**1949** ..........Minneapolis Lakers 4, Washington Capitols 2

## Who Won the Stanley Cup in...

**1940** ..........New York Rangers 4, Toronto Maple Leafs 2
**1941** .........................Boston Bruins 4, Detroit Red Wings 0
**1942** .................Toronto Maple Leafs 4, Detroit Red Wings 3
**1943**..............................Detroit Red Wings 4, Boston Bruins 0
**1944**................Montreal Canadiens 4, Chicago Blackhawks 0
**1945** .................Toronto Maple Leafs 4, Detroit Red Wings 3
**1946**......................Montreal Canadiens 4, Boston Bruins 1
**1947** ......Toronto Maple Leafs 4, Montreal Canadiens 2
**1948**........................................Toronto Maple Leafs 4, Detroit Red Wings 0
**1949**........................................Toronto Maple Leafs 4, Detroit Red Wings 0

## The Buzz

RED SMITH   THE YANKEE CLIPPER   JOLTIN' JOE
BRONX CHEER   TED WILLIAMS
DIZZY DEAN   THE NEGRO LEAGUE   BROOKLYN DODGERS
LEROY "SATCHEL" PAIGE   THE BROWN BOMBER   JOE DIMAGGIO

**1940** • Tom Harmon leads the Michigan Wolverines to victory over Ohio State

**1941** • Horse racing's Triple Crown is won by Eddie Arcaro on Whirlaway
• Joe Louis knocks out Billy Conn in the thirteenth round of the World Heavyweight Championship
• Ted Williams' batting average is .406—the last time any major leaguer will hit over .400

**1942** • President Franklin D. Roosevelt gives baseball the go-ahead to play despite World War II
• FDR encourages more night baseball so that war workers may attend

**1943** • Chicago Cubs owner Philip K. Wrigley started the All-American Girls Professional
Baseball League, as the draft continued to deprive baseball of the best players

**1945** • The Brooklyn franchise withdraws from the NFL to join the new All-America Football Conference
• Maurice Richard is the first NHL player to score 50 goals in one season
• Baseball writers fail to elect a new Hall of Famer; no player gets the required three-fourths of the vote

**1946** • Los Angeles Rams sign the first black athletes to play in the NFL in the modern era
• Football rivals Notre Dame and Army play to a scoreless tie
• A new professional league is established, called the Basketball Association of America (BAA),
the forerunner of the NBA

**1947** • Jackie Robinson breaks baseball's "color barrier"

**1948** • Horse racing's Triple Crown is won by Citation, with Eddie Arcaro up
• Germany and Japan are not invited for the Summer Olympic Games held in London, although Italy is
• The Frisbee is invented
• An LA Rams player paints horns on his helmet—the first helmet emblems in pro football

**1949** • NHL goaltender Bill Durnan sets a shutout record of 309:21 minutes
• The New York Giants sign their first black players
• Jackie Robinson becomes the National League MVP
• Fausto Coppi is the first cyclist to win both the Tour and the Giro in the same year

A DECADE OF SPORTS

# Life Just Wouldn't Be the Same Without...

- ▸ Automatic Washers
- ▸ Electric Clothes Driers
- ▸ Blood Tranfusions
- ▸ Aluminum Foil
- ▸ Timex® watches
- ▸ Dacron
- ▸ Reclining Chairs
- ▸ Padded Dashboards in Cars
- ▸ Lego® Building Blocks
- ▸ Polaroid Camera
- ▸ Electric Typewriters
- ▸ Television
- ▸ Tupperware®
- ▸ Transistor
- ▸ Slinky
- ▸ Velcro®
- ▸ Penicillin
- ▸ LP record

## Remember These?

- • Icebox
- • Wringer Washer
- • Party Lines
- • hand cranked wall phone

## The Buzz

CYBERNETICS

EARLY-WARNING RADAR

DDT

THE A-BOMB

UNIVAC

LOS ALAMOS, NEW MEXICO

ROSWELL, NEW MEXICO

BIKINI ATOLL

J. ROBERT OPPENHEIMER

INTERCONTINENTAL BALLISTIC MISSILE

THE MANHATTAN PROJECT

UFO

# PARTY PLANNING CHECKLIST

### THREE WEEKS BEFORE:

- [ ] Plan the occasion > *a 40s nostalgia party*
- [ ] Create a compatible guest list
- [ ] Choose a location that will accommodate the number of guests
- [ ] Send invitations [date, time (start/end), place, directions] > *Ask guests to dress in clothing of the era*
- [ ] Plan and select decorations > *This can include old yearbooks, record albums and other memorabilia*
- [ ] Begin collecting materials and creating props
  > *Visit garage sales for old 45s and LPs, even old clothes* > *Movie memorabilia stores are good sources*
- [ ] Prepare menu and grocery list > *Consider using food from the era for extra nostalgia*
- [ ] Select and hire caterer/serving help (if using)

### A FEW DAYS BEFORE:

- [ ] Call any guests who have not responded
- [ ] Buy groceries and beverages
- [ ] Prepare and refrigerate/freeze food items that can be made in advance
- [ ] Make party costume or select outfit

### ONE DAY BEFORE:

- [ ] Clean house, party room facility or other party site
- [ ] Set up and arrange party room
- [ ] Thaw out frozen party foods
- [ ] Get out serving pieces
- [ ] Coordinate last-minute arrangements with caterer, servers (if using)

### THE DAY OF:

- [ ] Decorate party room
- [ ] Prepare and arrange remaining food
- [ ] Coordinate set-up, service, cleanup with hired helpers (if using)
- [ ] Mentally travel through party > BEGINNING: *arrivals and introductions* > MIDDLE: *food and activities; have everyone sign the book* > END: *wrap it up! Party favors, Polaroid photos*
- [ ] Dress in party outfit
- [ ] Await guests
- [ ] Have a good time!

# HAPPY DAY!

Hope You Enjoyed Your Party...We Sure Did!

For additions, deletions, corrections or clarifications in future editions of this text, please contact Paul Shepherd, Senior Acquisitions and Development Editor for Elm Hill Books.

Manuscript written and compiled by Jamie Chavez.

Layout and design created by Susan Rae Stegall of D/SR Design, LLC.

Front cover photo by Jackson DeParis Photography.

Music tracks courtesy of Everest Records